A LOOK AT MONEY MATTERS

BUDGETS

BY ROSIE BANKS

CRASHCOURSE

Gareth Stevens PUBLISHING

Please visit our website, www.garethstevens.com. For a free color catalog of all our high-quality books, call toll free 1-800-542-2595 or fax 1-877-542-2596.

Library of Congress Cataloging-in-Publication Data
Names: Banks, Rosie, 1978- author.
Title: Budgets / Rosie Banks.
Description: Buffalo, NY : Gareth Stevens Publishing, [2024] | Series: A look at money matters | Includes index.
Identifiers: LCCN 2023023724 (print) | LCCN 2023023725 (ebook) | ISBN 9781538292259 (library binding) | ISBN 9781538292242 (paperback) | ISBN 9781538292266 (ebook)
Subjects: LCSH: Budget--Juvenile literature. | Money--Juvenile literature.
Classification: LCC HJ2005 .B36 2024 (print) | LCC HJ2005 (ebook) | DDC 352.4/8--dc23/eng/20230621
LC record available at https://lccn.loc.gov/2023023724
LC ebook record available at https://lccn.loc.gov/2023023725

First Edition

Published in 2024 by
Gareth Stevens Publishing
2544 Clinton Street
Buffalo, NY 14224

Designer: Leslie Taylor
Editor: Therese Shea

Photo credits: Cover (cell phone) Prostock-studio/Shutterstock.com; cover & Series Art (background) creativenv/Shutterstock.com; Series Art (falling coins) Abscent Vector/Shutterstock.com, (moneybag) VectorArtist7/Shutterstock.com; p. 5 BearFotos/Shutterstock.com; p. 7 Linaimages/Shutterstock.com; p. 9 IconicBestiary/iStockphoto.com; p. 11 Daniele Mezzadri/Shutterstock.com; p. 13 Warongdech Digital/Shutterstock.com; p. 15 fizkes/Shutterstock.com; p. 17 TarikVision/Shutterstock.com; p.19 kitzcorner/Shutterstock.com; p. 21 Shcherbakov Ilya/Shutterstock.com; p. 23 Lane V. Erickson/ Shutterstock.com; p. 25 Bob Korn/Shutterstock.com; p. 27 Judd Irish Bradley/Shutterstock.com; p. 29 TJ Brown/Shutterstock.com.

Printed in the United States of America

CPSIA compliance information: Batch #CW24GS: For further information contact Gareth Stevens at 1-800-542-2595.

CONTENTS

Words in the glossary appear in **bold** type the first time they are used in the text.

BUDGET, THEN BUY

Everyone needs to spend money sometimes. Most people should think before they buy. They should make sure they have enough money. And they should make sure they have enough money for other needs too. They need a plan called a budget.

MAKE THE GRADE

Budgets aren't just for adults. Younger people can use budgets to save for things they want.

WHAT IS A BUDGET?

A budget is a written plan that helps people decide how and when to spend their money. To make a monthly budget, they need to know their monthly income, or how much money they earn each month. They also need to know their monthly expenses.

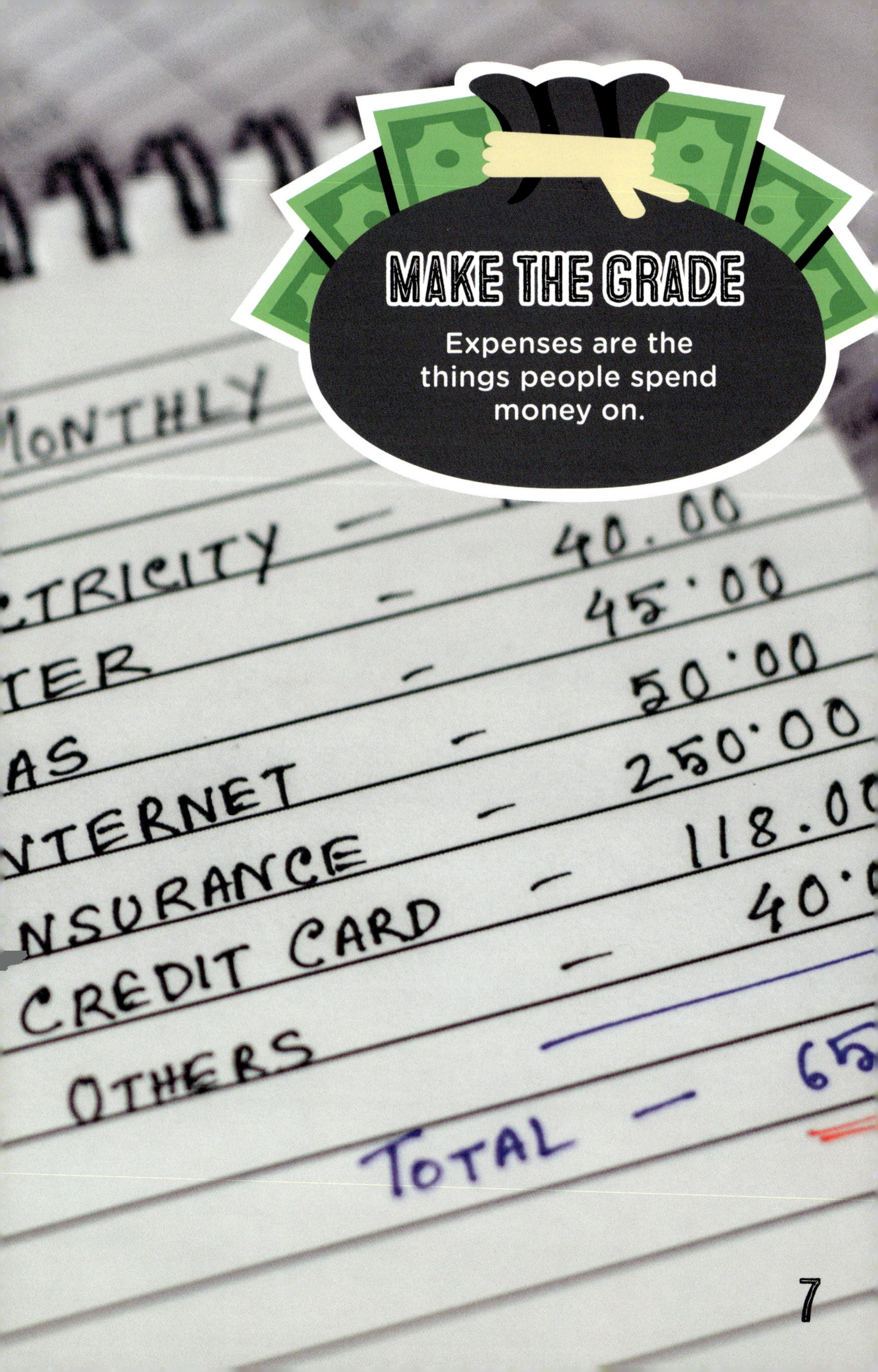

MAKE THE GRADE

Expenses are the things people spend money on.

A PERSONAL BUDGET

Math can help a person figure out if a budget works. They subtract the cost of expenses from their income. Check out the monthly budget on the next page. This budget works because the income is greater than the expenses. There is money left over.

MAKE THE GRADE

A person can budget to fit their needs. A weekly budget might make more sense for somone who gets paid weekly.

If a person runs out of money before the end of the month, the budget doesn't work. They will need to make a new one. If they can't make more money, they will need to spend less.

MAKE THE GRADE

After expenses are paid, it's OK to "break even." That means to not have any money left over. However, a person can use leftover money for **emergencies** or for savings.

MONTHLY BUDGET
• INCOME 2 000
GAS 400
ELECTRICITY 400
GROCERY 350
TELEPHONE 50
RENT 500
FUEL 200
CLOTHES 200
CAR 250
-350
SPEND LESS!!!
EARN MORE

NEEDS AND WANTS

People must know the difference between needs and wants to make their budget work. Needs are things necessary to live. They include food, a home, and clothes. Wants are things that people would like but can live without. A budget must pay for needs first.

MAKE THE GRADE

Candy, toys, and games are wants, not needs.

CHANGING WITH THE TIMES

People's needs and wants change over time. This means budgets should change over time too. It's important to **adapt** to changes. People whose budgets go over their income can go into debt. Debt is money owed. Not fixing a budget can make a debt grow larger.

MAKE THE GRADE

Credit cards are a way to borrow money. They can lead to greater debt if not paid off each month.

THE 50/30/20 BUDGET

Many people suggest a 50/30/20 budget. Each number stands for a **percentage**. If you earn $100, 50 percent, or $50, would cover needs. Then, 30 percent, or $30, could buy wants. Finally, 20 percent, or $20, would be put into savings.

MAKE THE GRADE

Savings can add up over time. They can help people pay for an expensive, or costly, want.

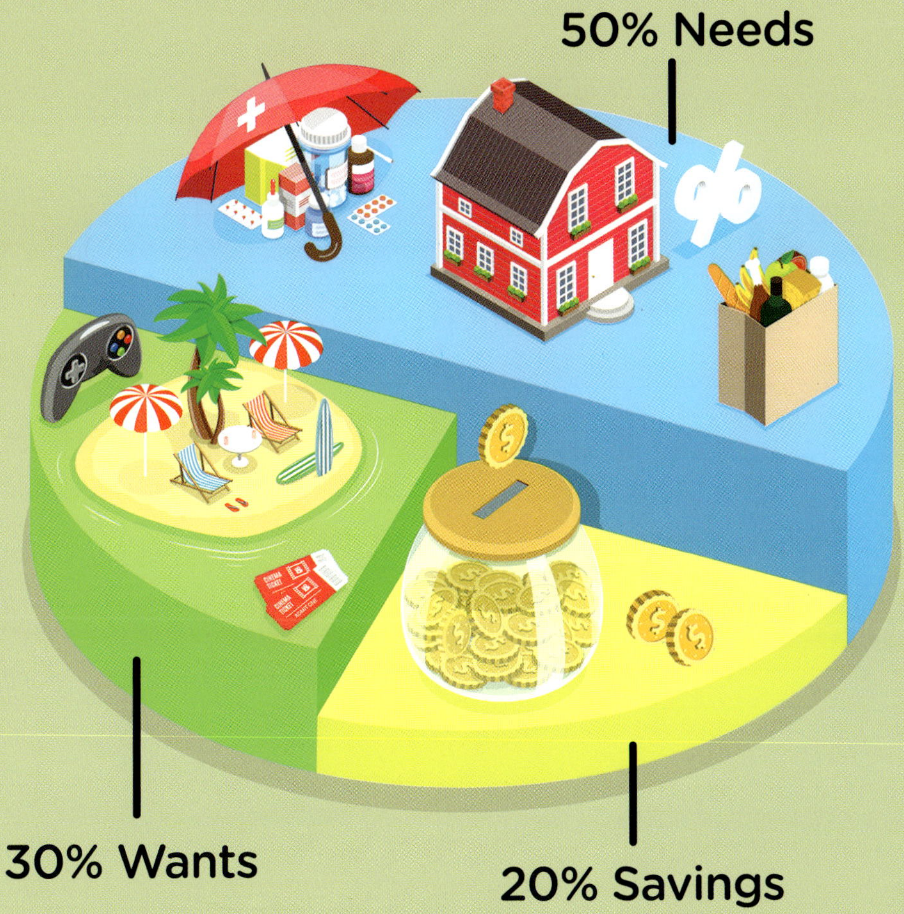

NOT JUST ONE

People can have several budgets! Many people make budgets for themselves. They make one for their families too. Business owners make budgets for their companies. They can save up to make improvements, to pay more workers, and to buy tools to make the business better.

MAKE THE GRADE

A person could also make a budget for a trip. They can decide what to spend their money on while they're away.

GOVERNMENT BUDGETS

Governments make budgets too. They decide how to best spend tax money. Local governments, such as towns and cities, need budgets to supply services without going into debt. So do larger governments, such as county and state governments. National governments make budgets too.

MAKE THE GRADE

A government budget is broken into smaller budgets. For example, there might be a budget for roads and a budget for libraries.

THE FEDERAL BUDGET

The U.S. federal, or national, government makes a budget each year. The budget has three parts. Mandatory spending is for the needs of the nation. These are in the budget under the law. Mandatory spending makes up about half to two-thirds of the budget.

MAKE THE GRADE

Mandatory means required by a law or a rule. This includes **Social Security** and health care programs. Mandatory spending was $4.1 **trillion** in 2022.

About one-fourth to one-third of the federal budget is discretionary spending. This money goes toward national **defense**, education, and much more. The smallest part of the federal budget goes toward paying off the **interest** on the federal government's debt.

MAKE THE GRADE

"Discretionary" means able to be used on things that are not thought necessary but are useful.

Passing a government budget isn't easy. Everyone has an idea about how money should be spent. Members of Congress want to help the causes and people they **represent**. It takes a lot of **debate** to pass the federal budget.

MAKE THE GRADE
The federal government's **fiscal** year goes from October 1 through September 30 of the next year.

COMPROMISE OR SHUTDOWN

Sometimes, the government can't agree on a budget on time. That can lead to a shutdown. During a shutdown, all discretionary spending is stopped until Congress reaches an agreement. Mandatory services continue. The government looks for a **compromise** to settle the budget for another year.

MAKE THE GRADE

Federal shutdowns close museums, libraries, parks, and any services considered not necessary.

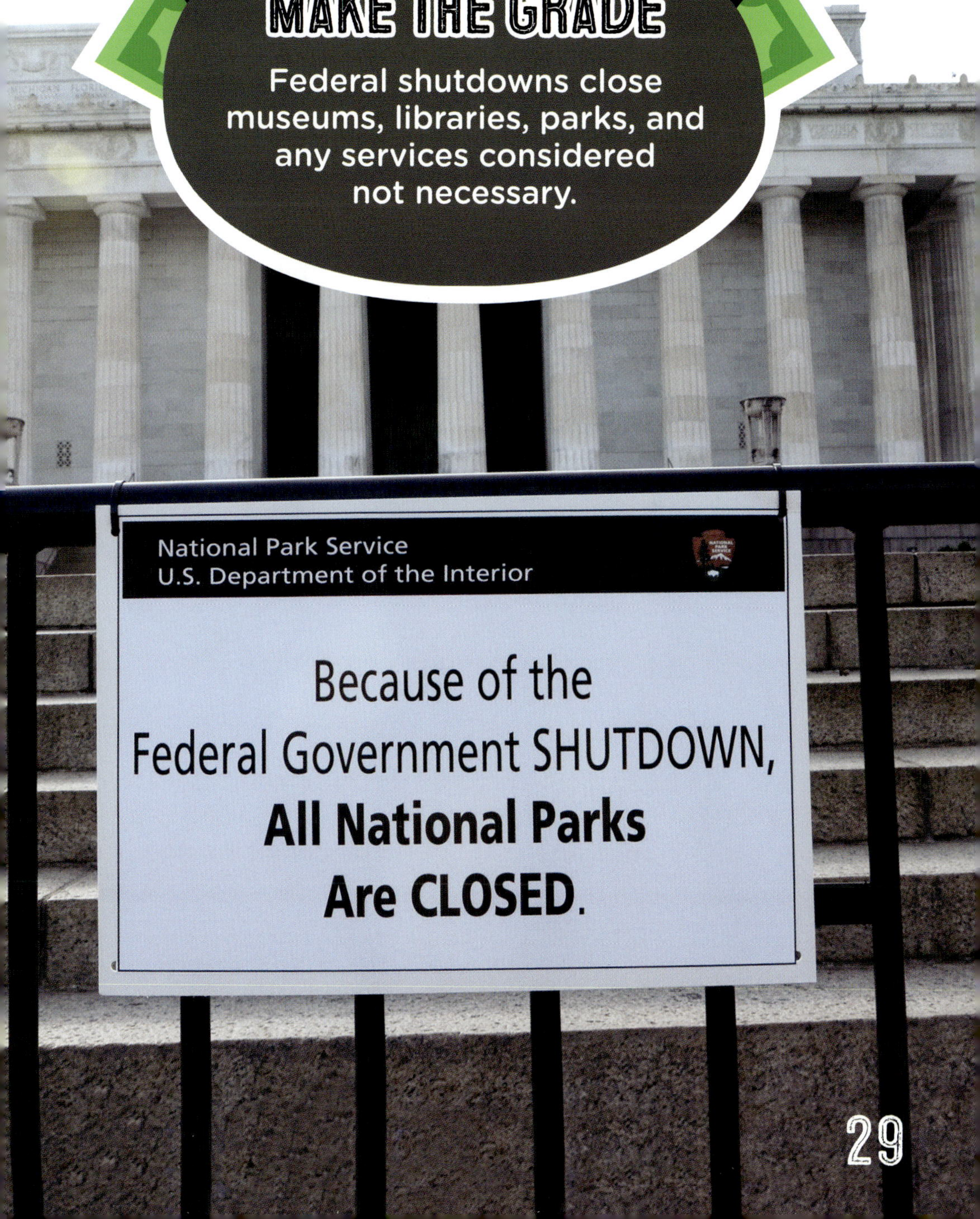

STEPS TO THE FEDERAL BUDGET

Federal agencies, or groups, make budget plans and give them to the White House Office of Management and Budget (OMB).

The OMB makes a budget for the president.

The president gives the budget to Congress.

Different groups called committees debate the funding for government needs and wants.

Congress makes a budget.

Congress sends funding bills to the president to sign.

GLOSSARY

adapt: To change to suit conditions.

compromise: A way of two sides reaching agreement in which each gives up something to end an argument.

debate: Having to do with a public discussion or argument.

defense: A way of guarding against an enemy.

emergency: An unexpected event that needs quick action.

fiscal: Having to do with money.

interest: Money paid to be able to use an amount of money that someone borrows.

percentage: A number that is expressed as a part of 100.

represent: To act or speak for.

Social Security: A U.S. government program that provides the elderly, those with disabilities, and some families with money to help meet their needs.

trillion: The number 1,000,000,000,000, or one thousand billion.

FOR MORE INFORMATION

BOOKS

Stratton, Connor. *Money Management.* Lake Elmo, MN: Focus Readers, 2023.

Uhl, Xina M., and Judy Monroe Peterson. *Making a Budget.* New York, NY: Rosen YA, 2020.

WEBSITE

Needs and Wants
www.kids.britannica.com/kids/article/needs-and-wants/630969
Find out more about needs and wants and how to decide what should go in your budget.

Publisher's note to educators and parents: Our editors have carefully reviewed these websites to ensure that they are suitable for students. Many websites change frequently, however, and we cannot guarantee that a site's future contents will continue to meet our high standards of quality and educational value. Be advised that students should be closely supervised whenever they access the internet.

INDEX